Bring Your Unique Purpose to Life

5 Practical Steps to Finding Clarity & Direction

by Joe Elliott

Copyright © 2023 by Joe Elliott

All rights reserved. No part of this publication may be reproduced, distributed or transmitted in any form or by any means, including photocopying, recording, or other electronic or mechanical methods, without the prior written permission of the publisher, except in the case of brief quotations embodied in critical reviews and certain other noncommercial uses permitted by copyright law. For permission requests, write to the publisher, addressed "Attention: Permissions Coordinator," at the address below.

Scripture quotations marked NIV are from *The New International Version*, New International Version®, NIV®. Copyright © 1973, 1978, 1984, 2011 by Biblica, Inc.™ Used by permission of Zondervan. All rights reserved worldwide. www.zondervan.com The "NIV" and "New International Version" are trademarks registered in the United States Patent and Trademark Office by Biblica, Inc.™

Scripture quotations marked ESV are from *The Holy Bible, English Standard Version*® (ESV®), copyright © 2001 by Crossway, a publishing ministry of Good News Publishers. Used by permission. All rights reserved.

Master Design Publishing
  an imprint of Master Design Marketing, LLC
32 N Gould St
Sheridan, WY 82801
www.MasterDesign.org

Bring Your Unique Purpose to Life / Joe Elliott. — 1st ed.

ISBN 978-1-941512-62-3 (Hardback)
ISBN 978-1-941512-63-0 (Ebook)

Printed in the USA

10 9 8 7 6 5 4 3 2 1

Acknowledgments

Thank you to all my friends, family, and supporters who have made this book possible. There really are too many of you to thank!

Special thanks to Harlie Alden for your graphic design work and patience, Laurie Garcia and Michelle Hiller for your early revisions and editing, and Kenneth Camp for your encouragement and vision to get this in the hands of those who need it most.

How to Use This Book

It's possible to fly through this book in a matter of hours. Maybe some of these steps are things you are already doing, and you mainly want to check your strategy against mine. There is nothing wrong with that; however, I would encourage you to do the exercises anyway. My best ideas have always come from taking the time to slow down and think.

My suggestion would be to go through one step per day. If you are pressed for time, then maybe one step every week. Consider doing this with a spouse or friend and taking time to share your answers with one another.

If you are a mentor and are guiding someone through this book, consider participating in the exercises with them. This content has been used to help juveniles, college students, successful business leaders, employees, celebrities, and influencers find a deeper sense of purpose.

Finally, we encourage you to write in this book. Getting your thoughts out on paper is important. You will likely reflect back on this material, so having what you were thinking written down will be valuable to you in the future.

Foreword

Some paths that I have crossed with people seemed fleeting at best, almost like a distant memory. Others, I have crossed paths with just once, but our journeys followed a congruent path from then on. The most prominent one being my wife of over thirty-five years.

But a few times in my life, my path continued to intersect with another as if someone purposefully kept rerouting me or them, perhaps both of us, because of a reason greater than either of us.

Joe has been one of these persons in my life.

When our paths first crossed, Joe was a youth pastor at a church in Austin while I was serving on another church staff in Austin as a missions pastor.

One of my earliest memories of Joe was at a pastor's retreat. Joe led a breakout session for other youth pastors. Joe is not a "let's keep doing the same thing" kind of guy. He led that group of youth pastors through an exercise that began with a question. He posed something like this:

"If you had unlimited resources and could do anything in your ministry to reach more teens and young adults, what would you do?"

The youth pastors shared many ideas, some way out of the box and others more traditional.

Joe stepped back and looked at the white board full of ideas and stated, "If we did half of these things in our ministry, we would all be looking for new jobs."

Probably true even if it is sad. And because of that, most returned to ministry as usual.

But not Joe.

Joe is not one who settles for business as usual. That pivotal retreat set Joe on a new path in his passion to reach the next generation.

That retreat was in 2011, if I remember correctly. Joe approached his senior pastor and shared his vision with him about how to reach teens that wouldn't even consider stepping inside a church. It would mean a radical shift in youth ministry.

That senior pastor gave Joe the green light, but eventually this radical approach launched into The Catalyst Collective, which developed what is now called The Purpose Project.

For the past twelve years or so, Joe and his team have perfected an approach of helping teens and young adults discover their unique design and how to live a life of purpose out of that design.

I personally have been involved with The Catalyst Collective and The Purpose Project for over two years as a friend, a consultant, an advocate, and a mentor (which they call a Purpose Project guide). I have used The Purpose Project with students as young as twelve to coaching clients of mine in their fifties.

What Joe and his team have developed and perfected with thousands of young people and old alike over the past ten years in many different settings works.

This book captures The Purpose Project method in a way that is easily understood and applied whether you are a parent, a youth pastor, a business owner, or a coach.

But here is the real purpose behind this book....

I encourage you, urge you, to invest in the next generation by becoming a mentor. Every teen and young adult is at-risk in today's world.

What they need is you.

This book will equip you with a proven method of mentoring that will take away any excuse you can come up with for not investing in the next generation.

Will you read it and answer the call?
Kenneth A. Camp
Business Coach
www.KennethACamp.com

Why This Book Is for You

After graduating college and spending nine years in technology sales, I had reached my breaking point. The money was good; the house and cars were great. My wife and I just had our third kid and all I kept thinking about was how much more money I needed to make. How was I going to do college for these kids, retirement, work in vacations, etc.?

At thirty years old, I was tired of chasing things and frustrated with the lack of guidance in my life. I never really had mentors growing up—just kind of figured things out by trying and failing. I hated my career, felt like my degree in management and marketing was a waste of time, and had no clue what I wanted to do next. My mortgage, car payments, and monthly bills felt like shackles. The only way I thought I could be happy was by continuing my career in sales to make more money and buy things that distracted me from the reality that I was not living a life authentically aligned to who I was made to be. I knew I was capable of more. There was something inside nudging me to take some risks and pursue a path that might unlock this hidden potential within.

My wife and I decided to take the first step in exploring the unknown by selling our house and half of everything we owned, downsizing into a small mobile home on the outskirts of Austin, Texas. We didn't know what would come next, but we knew at least we would be more flexible and ready.

Over the next fifteen years, we launched a ministry with $500 per month operating capital that turned into a successful non-profit, and eventually led to the awakening of a dream in our now family-owned retreat business called Wild Roots in Lockhart, Texas. This book, however, is not about the details of our journey so much as it is about the practical steps that were taken to go from frustration to fulfillment. We have had the privilege of helping thousands of people discover their unique design and purpose on this journey, and this book outlines the five most practical steps you can take to unlock the potential and passions within yourself.

As I sit down to write this book, I do my best to be encouraging, but trying to inspire you is not the goal. I want you to complete this book having absolute clarity on who you were born to be and what exactly to do about it. The steps outlined are as practical as it gets and invite you to reflect on how you must apply them to your journey. The best part is you are not alone. I have an entire community of mentors standing by, waiting to help you move forward faster.

If you are tired of settling, this book is for you. If you have grown weary of thinking about making a change in your life and are ready to have someone guide you on how to do it, this book is for you. If you know you will regret not taking more risks and desire to tap into the best parts of who you are, this book is for you.

There will never be a perfect time to make a change in your life. That illusion will keep you exactly where you are. It's normal to fear the future at times, but fear is an emotion that is not permanent. I believe that if you follow the steps we outline, you will find yourself in a place of hope and possibility. It is never too late to invest in yourself and this book will show you how to do it like a pro.

I truly believe your best is yet to come.

Table of Contents

Your Blueprint — xiii

Step 1: Debate Your Purpose — 1

Step 1 Notes — 10

Step 2: Discover Your Purpose — 13

Step 2 Notes — 29

Step 3: Develop Your Purpose — 33

Step 3 Notes — 49

Step 4: Work Your Purpose — 53

Step 4 Notes — 69

Step 5: Perfect Your Purpose — 73

Step 5 Notes — 88

Your Blueprint

5 Practical Steps to Finding Direction & Confidence in Life

Overview

Step 1: Debate Your Purpose

In this step, we will set the stage by:
- Exploring the concept of purpose
- Addressing the adversity that comes with opportunity

Step 2: Discover Your Purpose

In this step, we will explore your unique design through the lens of your:
- Life experiences
- Natural talents
- Personality type
- Values & Motivators
- Passions
- Themes & Purpose Statements

Step 3: Develop Your Purpose

In this step, you will learn how to:
- Choose a path in life you love
- Develop a legacy vision and set yourself up for long-term success
- Create short-term goals and strategic actions around your path
- Build a team to help you
- Conduct a Personal SWOT Analysis to guide you

Step 4: Work Your Purpose

In this step, you will learn how to:
- Manage your time like a pro
- Avoid financial pitfalls
- Transition from your current job
- Embrace the principle of learning by doing

Step 5: Perfect Your Purpose

In this final step, we will encourage you to:
- Become a student of life
- Avoid the things that take most people out
- Embrace failure and adversity
- Stay focused and motivated
- Enjoy the ride

Step 1:
Debate Your Purpose

Step 1: Debate Your Purpose

Whether or not you loved science as a subject in school, you were introduced to a process of exploring the world around you called the Scientific Method. It started with a question, followed by some research into the subject which led to a hypothesis. From there, you conducted an experiment, made observations, and came to a conclusion. While it may have been a few years since you have been a part of any science experiments, the Scientific Method is very much alive in your quest for clarity on a regular basis.

What Is My Purpose?

This is a HUGE question and one that requires some research and experimentation. Researching careers might be helpful or overwhelming. Exploring avenues of faith could provide general guidance but will likely not bring you the precise answer you are looking for. Knowing WHY you exist is different from knowing WHAT you exist to specifically do. So, let's start with what we know about ourselves as humans.

As far as we know, we do not yet live inside a matrix like the 2000 movie starring Keanu Reeves would suggest with machines controlling our minds and bodies. Instead, we have various levels of freedom to make choices every day on how we act and live. We also know that we all have different life experiences, talents, passions, values, motivators, personality types, and more. Each one says something very important about our unique design and provides clues as to what sets us apart from one another. With this freedom and diversity comes the opportunity to do something we were never taught how to do in school—apply the scientific methodology to achieve clarity and confidence about our unique design and why it matters. As we work through this process together, we will study your design to make some key observations that will help you embrace your unique purpose in a fresh way.

Within you exists a mix of natural qualities that are designed to be used in collaboration with others' gifts to make a difference in the world around us. There are endless possibilities of what can be done with what you have been given so our goal will be to narrow that down to a handful of very exciting options.

Before you move on, take some time to reflect on any hunches or random thoughts you have had over the years regarding your job or career. Maybe you saw someone online or at an event and thought, "I bet I could do their job." Perhaps you have had some random business ideas, the desire to apply for a job you didn't think you would qualify for, or have heard people tell you about a career you would be great at. All these ideas are worth writing down even if you never do anything about them. If you have some current passions brewing inside you, make sure they make the list too!

Step 1
List 7 hunches you have had in your life regarding a potential endeavor

Step 2
Now rank them in order
(1 being the strongest urge and 7 being least compelling)

Step 3
Looking only at the top 3 from step 2, list some things those jobs or careers have in common

The way you are uniquely made is pre-wired to find great success in hundreds of different careers, roles, and situations—more than you can pursue in your lifetime. This is not a guarantee of success, but it is important that you know and believe that the foundation to do something great already lies within you.

Before I bought my house, I learned that it was pre-wired for a security system. I thought that meant it was all ready to go when I moved in, but it wasn't. The wiring was in place, but it still needed someone to come out and make all the contacts, install the control panel, and connect it to a live monitoring system. For my security system to function as it was designed, it required the influence and skills of many technicians, salespeople, and call center operators.

Like my pre-wired security system, you are an unfinished product that will require the right team around you connecting all the amazing pieces that make you, you! Nothing great is ever accomplished alone, so you are going to have to wake up every day and choose to put in work with the freedom you do have.

Before we dive in further, I want to provide you some guidelines I try to live by in order to continually step into the things I desire to accomplish. These principles will help you develop resilience which is exactly what you will need to bring any vision of the future to life. Here they are in no particular order.

Here is an example of what it looks like for me:

1. **I start my day by choosing to be grateful.** Our attitude shapes our actions, and I cannot afford to lose perspective

on how short life is. The opportunities I have to do something meaningful for others require me to be in the right headspace.

2. **I attempt to expect the unexpected each day and respond appropriately.** Has anyone ever had a day when everything went perfectly according to plan? I haven't. So, it makes sense to be prepared for adversities as well as new opportunities by simply spending sixty seconds to think about what might go wrong and what my plan will be if it does.

3. **I focus on the one thing I need to accomplish that day**—and I give it the majority of my energy.

4. **I remind myself to enjoy the ride.** There are thousands of things buzzing around us daily that can suck the joy out of life. Even when things are really bad, I know that there is value in failure and pain. This empowers me to take risks, speak boldly, give whatever I have in me to give that day, and just enjoy the rollercoaster of life.

5. **I do my best to encourage and thank those around me.** I admit that this is a muscle group I am still developing. The environment of people we choose to surround ourselves with influences who we are and what we become. It's hard to find relationships with others that bring out the best in you. When you do find them, nourish those relationships the best you can.

6. **I realize I can never be all things to all people.** When who I am and what I do is not a good fit for someone in need, I acknowledge it and move on. The more self-aware you become the more you will learn to position yourself in situations that will help you thrive.

7. **I end the day by choosing to be grateful again.** I already battle with pride as is, so I don't need to go to bed every night with a Superman complex. When our pride starts to swell, our humility retreats. Humility is the glue that keeps us moving forward despite our circumstances.

These seven habits are something I have been cultivating for some time, and I pray, will never stop. They provide a framework for me to go out and be the person I have been uniquely made to be. Now before we jump into how this will all play out specifically for you, I have one more very important thing for us to think about. War.

Making the Most of Every Opportunity

You said "yes" to this book experience, because at the end of the day, you want to live a life that truly matters. You know that you are willing to learn, willing to be challenged, and ready to put this all into practice. What you really need to know is that there are forces in life focused on making sure that none of this ever happens.

WHY?

Because we are at war.

No, I don't believe i am being too dramatic. Any human can look at this broken world we live in with pain, suffering, despair, violence, etc., and see that something is not right. Sometimes the battles are external and sometimes they are internal. As is the case for any war, it is imperative that we know our enemy and where the attack might come from.

When you said "yes" to being on this journey, you enlisted yourself in boot camp. Not everyone makes it through boot camp, but those that do are ready to take the fight to the next level. In a world that is hungry for hope, your quest to embrace and refine who you were made to be matters.

Let's take a quick look at some of the most common situations you likely have or will wrestle with as you explore your unique design.

1. **Doubt**

It's the oldest trick in the book, literally.

Remember the Genesis story of the devil questioning Eve's reasoning in the garden? He planted a seed of doubt about whether she understood God's words correctly. Doubt plagues all humans and infiltrates all aspects of life. We doubt our parenting, our relationships, our work, our faith, our thinking, our talent ... on and on.

Doubt will stop you from applying anything you learn on this journey. To overcome doubt, you must lean on the ancient definition of faith that states:

"Faith is confidence in what we hope for and assurance about what we do not see" (Heb. 11:1-3 NIV).

Your confidence and assurance come NOT from everything working out exactly as you hope. That will rarely, if ever, happen.

Your confidence and assurance comes from knowing that you have made a commitment to develop your gifts and passions and never quit. Ultimately, your success lies in your ability to keep moving forward DESPITE YOUR DOUBTS.

2. Endurance

If you clear the hurdle of doubt, your stamina will be under attack—with the devil banking on the hope that there will only be so much adversity you can take before you quit. To battle against this, you must always have the end in mind.

Let me give an example:

One common theme I found in my passions was the desire to help others find direction. I eventually set very specific goals about who I wanted to help, how and where, but this is not the end I had in mind. My goal was to be a wiser and more selfless person. This would require me to always be learning and connected to the needs of those around me.

Every day I wake up and face a new set of challenges preventing me from doing this. And, if I allow myself to become discouraged in the present, I take my eyes off the future. The only way I fail is by quitting.

So, if everything I desire to do in this life falls apart, I will be disappointed—yes. However, I will have in my possession the one thing that cannot be taken from me—my choice to have stayed the course and never quit.

3. Environment

A famous podcast I listen to, *Entrepreneur on Fire*, ends every episode with an encouraging challenge. The host, John Lee Dumas, tells his listeners that they are the average of the type of people they spend the most time around. We see this truth play out in many aspects of society, and it's largely true. You are who you hang around. If you desire to take all your talent and see it thrive, you must plant it around others who will water it.

Surrounding yourself in a nurturing environment will not happen overnight. You will need to be patient; you will need to network and develop new contacts, and you will need to try things you have never tried before.

4. Past Failures

Yep, you got plenty of them. We all do! If I were trying to prevent you from moving forward in life, I would want to get you stuck reliving your past mistakes. Any time you attempt something new, I would be right there to remind you that you will fail again, just like you did last time. Maybe even worse.

Overcoming this trap is easier said than done. Mistakes are vital to your future success. They are our greatest teachers. They invoke emotion in us, and that emotion is a powerful motivator. For some, when reflecting on past mistakes, the emotion of fear rises to the surface. For others, determination flares up. One of these emotions works for you—the other against you.

Past failures bring humility into your life. Humility is a powerful weapon in war. With humility, you can glance into the past and choose gratitude that you not only survived those failures, but you grew in character as a result.

One More Thought

Life is too short to not be all in. You are embarking on the ultimate debate with yourself over the direction you want your life to take. It is healthy to wrestle with ideas on what is possible and strategies on what to do next. Once you pick a direction, however, you must commit to being all in for at least three to six months. Give yourself enough time to overcome early obstacles and decide whether the path you have chosen is worth pressing forward on. If it's not, redirect it by setting goals around a different path.

This first step is not the time to settle on your path. You will do that in Step 3. This first step exists to get you thinking and wrestling with some important concepts. In this next step, we will do the hard work of first looking at key aspects that make up who you are and the themes within you that you may be overlooking or taking for granted.

Notes:

Step 2:

Discover Your Purpose

Step 2: Discover Your Purpose

Have you ever seen someone work a puzzle with no strategy at all? Consider how strange of a sight it would be to watch someone dump a box of pieces on the table, pick up two random pieces to see if they fit and drop them back into the same pile if they don't. No sorting the edge pieces, no sorting into colors, not even spreading them out on the table. Weird, right?

Ironically, the strategy we often apply to discovering our path in life is not much different. We catch a glimpse of something we think we might be interested in and then spend tens of thousands of dollars exploring it in college or years and years working a job we knew we didn't like after the first month only to look back with regret on the amount of time and money we wasted. Life pressures us to often think and act quickly without providing us much guidance in the process.

As we begin to examine a different strategy for decoding our unique design, we will look at six core puzzle pieces that speak volumes into our identity. Those pieces include our life experiences, personality type, talents, values, motivators, and passions. While we are more complex than these six elements, we have found that these areas are the ones most worth exploring to understand what is at someone's core. Only then can we begin to make well-educated decisions on the potential paths you should be on.

We will walk you through each one, give you time to reflect, and then put them all together through a process of thematic analysis, which will point to the themes and core strength in your unique design.

Life Experiences

I am bowlegged. It's not super obvious, but I hate it. It seems that all my years of playing soccer gradually made a permanent dent in how I walk today. At the same time, all my years of soccer have led me to a place where I coached my daughter's competitive teams providing me the opportunity to invest in her development both on and off the field.

There is no denying our life experiences impact us: sometimes positively, sometimes negatively—and as is the case for me with soccer—sometimes both.

So, what do our life experiences have to say about who we are today and where we might be headed? First, our values in life are often formed because of our life experiences. Second, our passions can also be a byproduct of what we encountered growing up.

The most important thing we can do is take an inventory of where we have been. Let's start with the positive. Starting from childhood and working up to where you are today, reflect on the people, accomplishments, events, or experiences that made a positive impact on you.

Briefly state what or who it was and why it had a positive impact on you.

⊕ **Most Impacting:**

Now it's time to do the same reflecting over the negative experiences in our life. For many of us, this is a road we would rather not travel back down, yet it is vital to the process of becoming self-aware. The most successful individuals in life are also the most self-aware.

As you again think through the people, events, and experiences, that have had a negative impact on your life at some point, you might have already experienced ways in which that adversity has been leveraged in a positive way.

For now, though, just take note of things that negatively impacted you at some point in life.

```
┌─────────────────────────────────────────────┐
│                                             │
│                                             │
│                                             │
│                                             │
│                                             │
├─────────────────────────────────────────────┤
│  ⊖  **Most Impacting:**                     │
│                                             │
│                                             │
│                                             │
└─────────────────────────────────────────────┘
```

Done. So, now what?

Well, nothing for right now. We will refer to this later. Use the space below to write down anything that stands out to you as you look back on both your positive and negative experiences.

Natural Talents

You are going to need a partner for this one—someone who knows you well. Don't try to cheat yourself by not getting someone else involved in this either.

Here is where our doubt flares up. We think we are good at something, but we're not sure. We have hunches, but not confidence. This is not the time to be humble, though. If you think you might have a talent for something, write it down. If you suck at it, that's why you got a friend involved to tell you.

On the flip side, your friend may also make you list things that they think you are good at, but you don't agree with their thoughts.

Write it down if they tell you to. You can put a question mark by it if it will make you feel better.

Quick Exercise – Natural Talent Inventory

Before you start, remember that a natural talent is just something that comes naturally to you. You can do it without a ton of effort. It could be a skill like fixing specific things, singing, acting, or writing. It could be more descriptive in nature, like listening, empathy, or patience. Think about any time someone has ever said, "You are good at _____," and write it down.

Don't stop until you have listed ten things. Then circle the top five that you feel most confident in.

1.	11.
2.	12.
3.	13.
4.	14.
5.	15.
6.	16.
7.	17.
8.	18.
9.	19.
10.	20.

Good.

Make sure you circle the top five talents that you feel are your strongest or could be your strongest. If you wrote a list without a friend's involvement, stop, and send them this text:

"Hey. I'm doing this purpose project thing, and it's making me ask a friend what my natural talents are. Here is the list I came up with. Which do you think are my strongest? Would you add anything I missed?"

Since that wasn't hard, let's keep the momentum going.

Personality Type

"Your vision will become clear only when you can look into your own heart. Who looks outside, dreams; who looks inside, awakes."[1]
Carl Jung

Carl Gustav Jung was a Swiss psychiatrist and psychotherapist who founded analytical psychology. His work has been influential, not only in psychiatry, but also in philosophy, anthropology, archaeology, literature, and religious studies. It would later provide the foundation for one of the world's most widely used and scientifically verified assessments known as the Myers-Briggs Type Indicator or MBTI.

This is not a test to see which Star Wars character you are. This is an exercise in further self-awareness.

Since there are sixteen different personality types and only one that concerns you, we thought it best to leverage a great free resource to keep the costs of this journey down and allow you the most insight into how you are wired.

At this point, we would like for you to visit www.16personalities.com to take a free MBTI assessment. Before you do that, we need to tell you something important that can influence the outcome of this assessment.

BE HONEST.

When we take these types of tests, we tend to answer by projecting who we would like to be or must be, but not who we really are. The MBTI is designed to assess our natural tendencies. You might currently be in a job or environment, like sales, that forces you to be an extrovert in many areas. Given your natural preference, however, you would rather not talk to many people. So, when asked to agree or disagree with a statement like:

"You find it difficult to introduce yourself to other people."

The salesperson in you might tend to disagree, but outside of work, you would agree. In that scenario, you would want to answer based on how you feel in normal situations, rather than what you have learned to be comfortable with because of a job.

Make sense?

---

1   "A Quote by Carl Jung," Goodreads, 2023. https://www.goodreads.com/quotes/7349754-your-vision-will-become-clear-only-when-you-can-look

The test takes fifteen to twenty minutes. Try not to mark anything neutral unless you feel strongly about being neutral.

Once the test is complete, read about your personality type and record the results in the chart below:

Type Strengths	Type Weaknesses

Four-Letter Type

One Sentence Description

Most people we have worked with over the years have felt this test has greatly helped them become more self-aware. Occasionally, we run into someone who will take the test and feel it is way off. If that is you, we would strongly recommend you go grab your friend again and retake the test with them at your side.

Remember, shortcutting any of this project is only going to hurt the level of clarity and direction you receive from this once we put it all together. Investing in yourself like this is not easy and takes time, but we promise it will lead you down the path you want to go.
You are doing great so far!

Values & Motivators

The qualities and values that matter to you the most are often qualities you look for in others you connect deeply with. Values can give us insight into the environments, careers, or opportunities we desire to be a part of, and some of the ones we might want to avoid.

Life is full of setbacks. When we feel like we have hit a wall, we need to understand the driving forces that will help us break through. Our motivators, much like our values, can help us create or discover the environments and circumstances that will draw out the best in us.

Look over the list of values we have provided and select the five that you feel best represent the qualities you find most important. Then look over the list of motivators and write down seven that you feel most frequently stir you to action.

Values:

Acceptance	Exploration	Productivity
Accountability	Family	Purpose
Achievement	Focus	Recognition
Adaptability	Freedom	Respect
Assertiveness	Fun	Responsibility
Balance	Generosity	Risk
Challenge	Gratitude	Security
Commitment	Hard Work	Selfless
Communication	Health	Service
Community	Honesty	Stewardship
Compassion	Hope	Support
Competence	Humility	Sustainability
Connection	Independence	Talent
Courage	Innovation	Teamwork
Creativity	Integrity	Tradition
Determination	Leadership	Transparency
Development	Learning	Truth
Discipline	Loyalty	Uniqueness
Efficiency	Motivation	Unity
Empowerment	Optimism	Vision
Enthusiasm	Organization	Wisdom
Equality	Passion	
Excellence	Patience	

Values

Motivators:

Autonomy – having freedom to be your own boss and work on your own.
Challenge – being faced with tackling big tasks or overcoming difficult obstacles.
Creativity – having time to explore, experiment, and discover new things.
Developing Others – the opportunity to lead and help others achieve their best.
Empathy – being able to understand what someone is going through and to help them.
Excelling – the opportunity to do quality work and exceed expectations.
Excitement – having a sense of adventure or risk in what you do.
Family – investing in your family and making them proud.
Friendship – the ability to develop strong relationships with others.
Fun – being a part of something that is lighthearted, making others smile.
Impact – taking part in something that is important and will make a difference.
Learning – the opportunity to grow and learn something new.
Money – earning something valuable in return for your effort.
Ownership – to be in charge and have influence over others.
Pressure – the adrenaline rush of having to complete something quickly.
Prestige – having or achieving something that others highly value or respect.
Problem Solving – finding solutions or solving problems for others.
Purpose – being a part of something meaningful and bigger than yourself.

Recognition – receiving acknowledgement or admiration for your work.
Service – the opportunity to generously give your time or talent to others.
Social Responsibility – the opportunity to speak out on or influence social issues.
Teamwork – working with others to achieve goals.
Variety – having a wider mix of responsibilities that keep things fresh and interesting.

```
┌──────────────── Motivators ────────────────┐
│                                            │
│                                            │
│                                            │
│                                            │
│                                            │
│                                            │
│                                            │
└────────────────────────────────────────────┘
```

Passions

You already got a head start on this in Step 1. This next question will either get you stirred up or frustrated. My wife hates it because she feels like she never has an answer that is as good as someone else's.

The good news is you can't get this question wrong. Give me a few minutes to frame this before I ask you though.

We already established that this world is jacked up (not that you needed our help to come to that conclusion). So, the passion question aims at drawing out which part of this broken world stirs in you the most.

This may seem like a big question, so I will just throw it out there, and we can break it down into pieces.

THE PASSION QUESTION: If you were given unlimited time, money, and resources, what would you do to make this world a better place?

BEFORE YOU ANSWER, KEEP READING!

Rule #1

When we say "unlimited time," you would still be bound to our 24-hour day. So, you couldn't fight every single injustice on earth, but you could make a serious dent in one particular area, especially when combined with all the money and resources you need.

Rule #2

Don't answer with your head—answer with your heart. Yes, access to clean water may be one of the largest problems our planet faces, but that may not necessarily be an issue you are super passionate about.

Rule #3

Review your life experiences. It may not be the case for you, but for many, our greatest pains do foreshadow our greatest passions. Consider how your experiences in life have influenced issues that matter to you in this world.

Okay, you can answer now. Write down a few areas that come to mind. What issue would you tackle? In what part of the world? What age group? Try to be specific.

Perhaps you have a history of mental illness in your family and that is an area you are passionate about seeing others healed in? That's a good start, but who, what types of illness, and where might you start?

That's being specific.

My Passions

Putting It All Together

Okay, now it's time to zoom back out and look at the big picture. Let's go back through the answers you gave and follow the directions to summarize everything on this one-page puzzle sheet.

As we wrap up Step 2, you have created a border around your purpose and sorted everything into sections. The problem is you don't have the box cover, just the pieces ready to be connected, so let's connect some pieces.

Life Experiences	Personality Type
Natural Talents	**Values**
Motivations	**Passions**

Connecting the Pieces with Three Simple Steps

With the data points collected regarding your unique design, we will begin our thematic analysis by coding words and ideas that may connect to each other. Coding is simply the process of marking words with either numbers or symbols.

First, begin by coding forms of words that match. For example, words like *create, creative, creating, creation* should all be coded the same.

Next, expand this by looking for synonyms related to these words. For example, words like *make, build, invent,* and *design*, would all be words that should fall under the same code. If you are using numbers for codes then I would mark everything that connects to the idea of building or designing with the number one. This would be your first theme.

Finally, read between the lines to see if this code is also present in ideas, feelings, or behaviors that were captured. An example would be that under life experiences you find a statement like "loved playing with Legos."

List some of the themes you have found here. If you are having trouble finding the themes, we can help you! Go to www.purposepro.org and sign up for a private session where one of our certified Purpose Project Guides will walk you through it virtually!

Common Themes

Purpose Statements

Before moving to Step 3, we have one more exercise for you. It's time to connect your themes to a passion with a purpose statement.

In drawing some conclusions, you may see that you are a highly creative person, who enjoys dealing with people face to face and has a passion to help them overcome traumatic pain in their life. Possible areas of interest could lie in art therapy, counseling, teaching underprivileged youth, or doing something new that nobody else is doing. Connect these themes and passion using a purpose statement like this:

"I can see myself doing _____ for _____, because I would be excited to see _____."

Specific Examples:

- I can see myself teaching guitar for adults, because I would be excited to see them embrace the idea that it's never too late to explore new passions.
- I can see myself starting a 24/7 teen center for all teens because I would be excited to see them have access to people who care about who they are and where they are going personally and professionally.
- I can see myself serving on the school board for my school district because I would be excited to see every student receive the best possible education experience our tax dollars can create for them.

Take some time to think through a few purpose statements of your own and write down at least three. You purpose statements will land on something that can be defined in one of three ways:

1. Completely new
2. Kind of like what you are doing or
3. A bigger step down the path you are already on.

This is where we will pick up in Step 3, because it is now time to narrow your focus. Before we move on though, I want to tell you that the vast majority of people on this planet never even get this far in the pursuit of their unique design and purpose.

YOU ARE DOING GREAT!

If you are not happy with the purpose statements you have crafted, we have a few options for you:

- Show five people your puzzle overview from this exercise and ask for their input on what themes they see and what purpose statement it might result in.
- Consider taking advantage of a one-hour coaching session with our team. We will look at what you have written down so far, ask you a bunch of questions, and help you think through possible purpose statements. To learn more about our options, go to www.purposepro.org.

If you are excited about some of the purpose statements you have written, it's time to move to Step 3, where we will help you **narrow your focus** and **create an action plan.**

Notes:

Step 3:

Develop Your Purpose

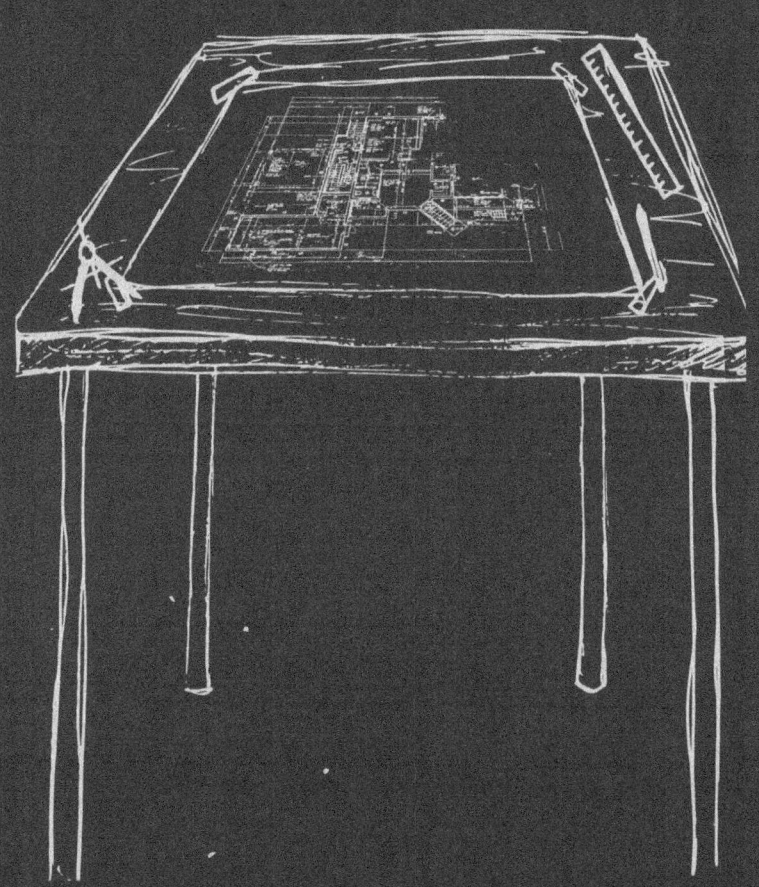

Step 3: Develop Your Purpose

It's now time to choose which purpose statement to pursue. If you are still afraid of making a "wrong" choice, it's probably a good time to remind you that the only wrong choice is not choosing any of them.

It is possible to start down a path only to later find out it's not the right one. You may be afraid of wasting time, money, and energy on something that may not work out. It's a risk and our natural inclination is to avoid risk.

But here's the problem: **you will never find success without risk.**

Risk is just part of the equation. Risk leads to failure and if you want to do something with your life that is meaningful, you will need to learn to embrace failure. The greatest risk of all, as many might argue, is to never risk failure at all.

Risk and Failure are your friends. (We will remind you of this in Step 4.) Risk and Failure are here to toughen you up. This is war, remember? This world needs people who can overcome their fears of failing and push forward anyway. That is what it means to be courageous.

You are a brave person already because you are willing to work through this book to contend for something more meaningful in your life. People think about making changes all the time but very few act. You are acting at this very moment even with uncertainty about your future circling all around you. You do have what it takes to be successful!

So, let's acknowledge our fears as being real because they will not completely go away, but they can be managed and even help us develop more courage, which is absolutely needed to bring our dreams into reality.

Evaluating Your Purpose Statements

It's best to have at least two, but no more than three, purpose statements. The following exercise will help you narrow this down to one. Number each purpose statement you created and score them using the following system.

Purpose Pathway

Confused on what pathway to pursue? Try this out. On a scale of one to ten with one being the lowest score and ten being the highest, answer these five questions for each purpose statement you have written out:

Passion
How excited do you get when you envision this purpose statement becoming a reality?

Opportunity
Do you have the resources you need to get started on this and has a pathway emerged for you to begin pursuing this purpose statement?

Skill
Do you have the natural talents needed to succeed at this?

Regret
How much will you regret never pursuing this purpose statement?

Sacrifice
To what level are you willing to endure hardship as you travel down this path?

Purpose Statement 1:

Scores:
Passion _____ + Opportunity _____ + Skill _____ + Regret _____ + Sacrifice _____ = _____

Purpose Statement 2:

Scores:
Passion _____ + Opportunity _____ + Skill _____ + Regret _____ + Sacrifice _____ = _____

Purpose Statement 3:

Scores:
Passion _____ + Opportunity _____ + Skill _____ + Regret _____ + Sacrifice _____ = _____

WINNER:

In the event of a tie, go with the one that you will most regret never going after, or that you would be willing to sacrifice the most for.

When we punch out of this life, we will all have regrets. Now is the time to decide which regrets you can live with and which ones you can't. If you pursue something and it does not work out, at least you will never have to live with the regret of not trying. To me, that is much worse than trying and coming up short.

It's extremely rare to hit a home run with your first attempt at something, but the more at-bats you give yourself, the higher the chances of eventually knocking one out of the park. Starting something new is always exciting. The excitement will come and go as the level of adversity you encounter increases, but that is all part of the journey.

You got this.

Take every thought captive right now that is causing doubt. You are making the most educated guess any human can make at this point when it comes to purpose and direction. You have already learned so much about how to self-evaluate that even if you stopped right here, you could still help hundreds of people get to the point you are at right now.

But you are not stopping…. This is only the beginning.

With your chosen purpose statement in hand, we are now going to create a life mission statement that will ensure your success before you ever even put any plans into motion.

Creating a Legacy Vision for Your Life

"What you get by achieving your goals is not as important as what you become by achieving your goals."[1]
Zig Ziglar

I'm so proud of you for not skipping this part! Your attention to detail is important and will be a significant factor in your success down the road.

---

1 "A Quote by Zig Ziglar," Goodreads, 2023. https://www.goodreads.com/quotes/145606-what-you-get-by-achieving-your-goals-is-not-as

A legacy vision statement is one or two sentences that describes how your life will influence others before it is over. Unlike your purpose statement that focuses on doing something, your legacy statement focuses on being something.

Here is mine:

> "To encourage those around me in their gifts and passions while providing opportunities for others to discover, develop, and pursue what matters most to them."

Others might be something like this:

> "To inspire people in their creative talents and help them live with hope despite having endured great despair."

> "To be the best student of history I can be, so that I may help others learn from the past and forge a better future."

A legacy vision is something that you want others to say about you after you are gone. In the business world, we call this beginning with the end in mind.

With a legacy vision in place, you are free to live it out in any number of possibilities. You can create purpose statements, pursue them, and even fall short, and it won't matter.

WHY? Because it's who you are being that really matters.

Steve Jobs, the founder of Apple, died before he was ready. Even though what he had accomplished was an enormous success, he still died with unfulfilled plans on the table. Now people will never know the things he might have brought to life if he had an extra ten years, but they will know how he inspired a generation to never give up on their creative ideas.

In the process of **doing**, Steve was **being** a person that was inspiring so many lives. We don't know exactly what his legacy vision was, or if he even had one, but we do know that he left behind a memorable legacy.

You and I may never influence as much of the planet as Steve Jobs, but that doesn't matter. What matters is that we have a legacy vision in place, so that when we evaluate our success in life it is being measured not as much by what we accomplish but rather by how we live.

There are so few role models in our world today because so few people live out (consistently) who they claim to be. Ask people why they no longer attend church, and many will point to Christians who have consistently modeled a life that counters that of Jesus. Ask teens why they don't respect their parents, or employees why they don't respect their bosses, and you will find the same type of response.

As humans, we desire to be led by others who can consistently (not perfectly) be the person we long to be.

So, what does this mean for **you**? Although we are giving most of the attention to finding and developing your purpose, your success in this life does not hinge on obtaining and fulfilling any one **specific** purpose.

Which is why establishing a legacy vision can help you stay aligned with what matters most. What do you want others to remember about the way you lived? Consistently choose to BE a person worth following and allow the cultivating of your specific path to express that as well as you can.

We are about to build a serious framework around your specific path, but I would encourage you to not move on before establishing your legacy vision. When you are ready, write it here:

My Legacy Vision

Creating Strategic Actions around Your Purpose Statement

"Setting goals is the first step in turning the invisible into the visible."[1]
Tony Robbins

If you have arrived at this part of your journey before solidifying your purpose statement and legacy, you are moving too fast. Being impatient in this process will come back to haunt you at some point.

---
1   Robbins, Tony. *Awaken The Giant Within.* Simon & Schuster Ltd, 2017.

Let's assume you are ready to go. How do you know you are taking the right steps down the path?

As you now move into the "experimentation" phase of The Purpose Project, you have made excellent observations that need to be tested in the field. Creating specific, short-term goals will help you take strategic action around bringing your unique purpose to life.

Sometimes we can set goals that are too easy to achieve. They don't challenge us or force us to develop our character. On the other hand, we don't want to create goals that are so challenging that we give up within the first few weeks. We will use the SMART goals framework to help us find the balance between easy and impossible. Each goal should be Specific, Measurable, Attainable, Relevant, and Timely.

A great place to start is simply by asking yourself if the goal you have will require you to be disciplined, sacrificial, and focused. If so, you are on the right track. The trick is to set the time frame around your goals to twelve weeks. Quarterly goals create a sense of urgency without stressing us out and can help us identify what we need to do on a weekly or even daily basis a little better.

Focus on Three Main Goals

In light of your purpose statement, what are the three most important things you need to accomplish first and can do so within twelve weeks?

```
┌────────────── My Three Main Goals ──────────────┐
│                                                  │
│                                                  │
│                                                  │
│                                                  │
│                                                  │
│                                                  │
│                                                  │
└──────────────────────────────────────────────────┘
```

To accomplish these goals, what strategic actions must you take over the next twelve weeks? HINT: they should be specific and measurable. Here is a template you can use....

SMART Goal #1

Deadline:

Strategic Actions

1. _____ 2. _____ 3. _____

Tasks that I will need to focus on to do this:

☐ _____ ☐ _____ ☐ _____

☐ _____ ☐ _____ ☐ _____

☐ _____ ☐ _____ ☐ _____

SMART Goal #2

Deadline:

Strategic Actions

1. _____ 2. _____ 3. _____

Tasks that I will need to focus on to do this:

☐ _____ ☐ _____ ☐ _____

☐ _____ ☐ _____ ☐ _____

☐ _____ ☐ _____ ☐ _____

SMART Goal #3

Deadline:

Strategic Actions

1. _____ 2. _____ 3. _____

Tasks that I will need to focus on to do this:

☐ _____ ☐ _____ ☐ _____

☐ _____ ☐ _____ ☐ _____

☐ _____ ☐ _____ ☐ _____

Before you take off, I want you to share a copy of this tracker with one or more people from your team.

What team?

The one you are about to assemble—because nothing great is ever accomplished alone.

Building Your Team

Having the right people hold you accountable to what you say you are going to do is a game changer. It may be the biggest factor that will determine your success now—and in the future—because nothing great is ever accomplished alone.

The American Society for Training and Development (ASTD) found that the probability of completing a goal increases as follows:
- 10% if you have an idea or a goal.
- 25% if you consciously decide you will do it.
- 40% if you decide when you will do it.
- 50% if you plan how you will do it.
- 65% if you commit to someone you will do it.
- 95% if you have a specific accountability appointment with a person you've committed to.

You are looking for two to five people (depending on the size of your goal) that can help challenge you, counsel you, and draw out the best in you. They must be knowledgeable, supportive, and able to tell you the hard truth. Each person you talk to **or get connected to will need to know three things:**

1. What it is you are trying to accomplish and why. (Share your purpose statement and SMART goals with them.)

2. How they can specifically help you.

3. How much of their time it will take to help you.

In order to communicate how they can specifically help you, consider these types of roles you might need:

Accountability/Coaching – Find someone who could meet with you to provide specific training or general advice.

Administrative Help – If your goal is way bigger than you, think about the types of help you might need and who would be great at organizing your events, marketing, handling money, doing paperwork, etc.

Encourager – Everyone needs that one person around them that is always positive. No matter how bad things get, having a cheerleader in your corner that is great at lifting you up will help you through the days where you want to give up.

But you don't know who these people are yet, do you? Most of us don't—which is why you must learn to network.

To be honest, I hate networking. As an INTJ personality type, my preference is not to interact with humans at all. I also know that the things I am passionate about have no chance of happening if I don't push myself out of my comfort zone daily. Networking is one of many ways I must do that.

The best place to start networking with people, so that you can draw closer to building your team, is to leverage social media. Start with Facebook, Instagram, or LinkedIn connections of people that are closer to you, and tell them what you are doing, and where you would love support.

When I did market research on teen centers a decade ago, there were none in my area, and the people I knew didn't know anyone I could connect with in that field, so I went to Google. I found teen centers across the USA, picked up the phone, and started talking to any of the founders or directors I could get a hold of. (https://alumline.source.colostate.edu/being-held-accountable-for-your-goals/)

I learned so much doing this. None of these people ended up being a permanent part of my team, but that's okay. When I shared the problem I was attempting to solve with people around me, several came forward and wanted to get involved. Many became my first board members.

As your goals change, so should some of the people you surround yourself with. So keep looking for people who can speak wisely in the areas you are focused on. Now here is something you need to remember: putting a great team around you takes time.

Make it your goal to develop your team within the first twelve weeks, but don't get frustrated if it doesn't happen. Be patient. Share your passion for the road ahead with others, and you will eventually cross paths with the people you want around you. Some hang around for months, and others, for years.

You have control over the networking piece of your strategy. Never quit trying to put the right people around you and be quick to remove those that derail your momentum. Your team is your own personal ecosystem; it's an environment designed to draw out the best in you, so develop and maintain it well.

Potential Team Members

Your Personal SWOT Assessment

I'm sure you are tired of self-analyzing, which is why this next segment will be something you are tempted to skip—but don't. Our team does SWOT assessments annually, and they create the blueprint for everything we do. That's how valuable they can be.

This evaluation has been around for quite some time, so while you may be familiar with it, you may not have completed one that focuses on your goals.

SWOT stands for Strengths, Weaknesses, Opportunities, and Threats. Most people draw it out like this:

Strengths	Weaknesses

Opportunities	Threats

We recommend taking yourself through this at least twice in the first year. Doing so will result in:

- Clarity of direction and purpose.
- Affirmation of what you are doing right.
- Identifying where you might need help.
- Being more aware of what is happening around you.

It also doesn't take very long to complete. Let me guide you through the four areas of assessment before you try it.

1. Strengths

As it sounds, strengths identify what you are doing well, or in the beginning, what you anticipate you will do well. Maybe you are highly disciplined—then, include discipline on this list. Maybe you love connecting with new people—then, include networking as well. Don't stop until you record seven to ten strengths that you have and that are relevant to your twelve-week goals. If you want to be a pilot, don't include the fact that you are a great cook.

2. Weaknesses

Same concept as above. Identify what you are not doing well, or what you anticipate not doing well, in relation to your current goals.

3. Opportunities

In light of what you are setting out to do, what are the biggest opportunities you need to take advantage of? If school is a required piece to achieving your specific goals, is there an opportunity to take at least one class this semester? Could you commit to attend a conference in the field you are interested in or interview others already doing what you want to do?

What if you desire to be an entrepreneur, and you already know a successful entrepreneur that is willing to mentor you? That's an opportunity. Anything that can advance your progress in achieving your goals is an opportunity.

List five to seven potential opportunities.

1.	5.
2.	6.
3.	7.
4.	

4. Threats

Great leaders are always glancing towards the horizon to see what is headed their way. There are always potential obstacles trying to take us out, and sometimes those hurdles are beyond our control.

Maybe you are battling an illness, and it is slowing your progress towards reaching your goals. Maybe your plan takes some startup capital, and you are not sure how to go about acquiring the money. Virtually anything can become a threat to your progress, so you want to evaluate some of the biggest potential threats that would keep you from pursuing your goals.

After you finish brainstorming these four quadrants, be sure to compile all your answers in the SWOT Analysis box we provided.

Okay, done. Now what?
- Address any imminent threats first. Seek wise counsel from others as to what you can do to avoid anything that might stop your progress altogether. The threats you identify should be reflected somewhere in your twelve-week goals or strategic actions.
- Make sure you have a plan in place to take advantage of the opportunities that are before you.
- Lean on your strengths and outsource your weaknesses. If administration is a weakness for you, find someone that can hold you accountable or volunteer to help you in this area. Focus the majority of your time operating in the things you do well, and find a way to navigate around your weaknesses.

The SWOT assessment can be a great tool in helping you see the big picture. We all suffer from tunnel vision at times. Try not to get so caught up in the daily grind that you miss what is happening at the one-thousand-foot level.

After completing your personal SWOT assessment, record your biggest takeaway from this exercise in the space below.

Notes:

Step 4:
Work Your Purpose

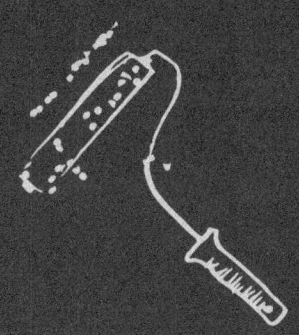
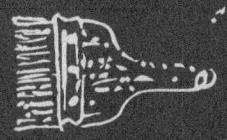
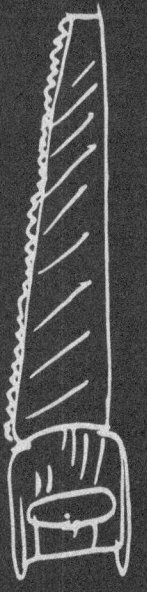

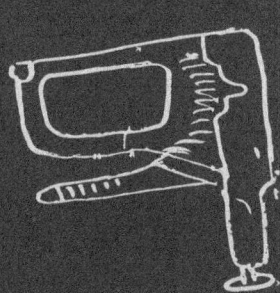

Step 4: Work Your Purpose

At this point you have wrestled with your desires and passions at a deep level, discovered key truths about what sets you apart, and developed a solid strategy that is now time to put to work.

The Urgent/Important Matrix

If I could turn back time to the start of my career, I would make someone teach me about the Urgent/Important Matrix. I think it would have simplified and focused my efforts in more ways than I can imagine.

In a speech to the Second Assembly of the World Council of Churches, former US President Dwight D. Eisenhower said: "I have two kinds of problems: the urgent and the important. The urgent are not important, and the important are never urgent."[1] This "Eisenhower Principle" is said to be how he organized his workload and priorities.

You cannot afford to overlook applying this to your life.

Before you begin, it is best to brainstorm all the things you do on a weekly or monthly basis. These are tasks you spend time doing or responsibilities you have. Then sort it using the parameters we have outlined for you here.

The Urgent/Important (Top Left)
These are all things that are both immediate and important. Your success hinges on giving focus to these areas with 80% of your time and effort.

The Not Urgent/Important (Top Right)
This is your long-term strategy section most likely. They are important for your success in the future, but ultimately they can wait because you have bigger fish to fry.

The Urgent/Not Important (Bottom Left)
These are all the annoying things that suck up your time, scream for your attention, but in the end, don't play a vital role in your success. Steven Covey calls them "time-pressured distractions."

---

1   Dwight D. Eisenhower. "Address at the Second Assembly of the World Council of Churches, Evanston, Illinois." The American Presidency Project, 2023. https://www.presidency.ucsb.edu/documents/address-the-second-assembly-the-world-council-churches-evanston-illinois

The Not Urgent/Not Important (Bottom Right)
In this section, you would put things that are good to do, but in light of everything else you listed, produce the least amount of return on investment. Often, these need to be delegated or completed in your dead time.

Once you complete this for yourself, I would print it out and post it somewhere where you are forced to look at it every day. It is way too easy for us to drift away from our focus. We can't even keep our hands off our cell phones when our car slows down in traffic. Our culture has made us busybodies that exert lots of energy, yet have little to show for it. So, go ahead and think through all that you have on your plate, and begin to sort them in your own Urgent/Important Matrix.

Your goals and strategic actions should reflect what is in the Urgent/Important section. If not, you need to either reconsider whether you have the right goals—or if the task is something that is both urgent and important. For those of you that believe EVERYTHING is urgent AND important, pull one of your team members in on this. Their outside perspective is very valuable.

	Urgent	Not Urgent
Important		
Not Important		

The Three Biggest Time Wasters

> "Yesterday is gone. Tomorrow has not yet come. We have only today. Let us begin."[1]
> **Mother Teresa**

If you are flying through this book and have gotten this far without skipping any steps, you probably feel more organized than you have felt in a long time.

That's great!

Let's keep you focused on your goals by addressing the three biggest things that suck your time away. Time management may be a natural talent of yours, but it's not for most of us. Even if you are great about controlling your schedule, you will still find areas you can adjust to create even more space to pursue your passion.

These three time wasters are after you. I wish there were only three, but if I gave you a list of one hundred you might get overwhelmed and quit before you start. You might have something that is not on this list, but it steals a lot of your time; if so, it's a threat and should be accounted for in your personal SWOT assessment.

Let's look at each of the three time wasters individually and assess the threat level they pose in your life.

1. Sleep

The average person spends one-third of their day asleep. Unfortunately, sleep is necessary, but if you are getting more or less than eight hours of sleep, something is robbing you of your time.

I have heard people say they NEED ten hours of sleep each night, when really what they NEED is a better diet and sleep schedule. If you are serious about pursuing a specific purpose in your life, you need to seriously consider what you are willing to sacrifice to attain it. Life does not care if you are a morning person, night owl, or something in between. If you are sleeping ten hours a day when you should be aiming toward eight, you are wasting 730 hours a

---

1 "A Quote by Mother Teresa." Goodreads, 2023. https://www.goodreads.com/quotes/44552-yesterday-is-gone-tomorrow-has-not-yet-come-we-have

year on something you can learn to do without. **That is an entire month you are throwing away every year just by sleeping!!**

Conversely, if you are averaging six hours of sleep per night, my question is why? Is it because you are working your butt off toward your goals, or is it because you spend too much time playing? If your lack of sleep is because of anything entertainment related or extracurricular, consider whether these activities are more important than the purpose statement you are pursuing.

2. Free Time

Like sleep, free time is something we all need to recharge and take a break from the norm. Some of us feel we have no free time, and others don't realize how much they actually have.

According to the Department of Labor Statistics, the average working American has four hours of free time per day, not including weekends. I think it's more like six to seven hours per day. Let me show you what I mean.

My alarm goes off at 6:00 a.m. Like you, I have to eat and get ready. I then have to go somewhere and sit in some traffic. When I settle at my desk, I check emails and get distracted by junk email and social media. Eventually, it will be time for lunch. Mid-afternoon will demand a break of some sort. When things are slow, back to social media. Then more time in the car traveling home or somewhere equally necessary. Each evening, I get around to the gym, dinner, binge watching, reading, time with kids, etc., before finally getting back into bed for another night's sleep!

If I had someone following me around with a stopwatch and asked them to mark down all the time I had free to do something related to my goals but didn't, what would they come up with?

3. Excessive Communication

I am the kind of person that likes to get straight to the point, but when I am passionate about a topic, I tend to get long-winded. We waste so much time communicating information that is just not necessary.

A phone call is often much faster than texting something that is hard to explain. A simple voice text is often faster than a long email explanation. We can get on a phone call with someone for a quick chat and find ourselves talking about the most random topic that has no value for either of us.

And I know all of us have been in an hour-long meeting that should have taken five minutes.

Don't get me wrong—it's important to build relationships with others, and sometimes our lengthy communication is really about getting to know the people around us. Most of the time, however, it's not. It seems that we all could benefit from applying the urgent/important philosophy to each of our methods of communication.

Convey what is urgent and important in the first few minutes of conversation or connection, as often as possible. Use discernment about whether a call, email, or text is most efficient. Be mindful of repeating things you have already communicated.

Stop treating your inbox as a trauma center. If you let the email sit there awhile, you may find that the problem solves itself. Not all communication is both urgent and important. Find a way to say no and politely end communication if it continues to drag on.

Your Top Three Time Wasters

Just talking about time management is helpful, but what does it look like in your world? Take a minute to consider the top three time wasters you encounter and changes you can make to earn back some of that valuable time.

My Time Wasters

What to Do about Them

After acknowledging these are threats to your future success, your goal is to be more mindful of them and set small goals for yourself by trying to build better habits in these areas. As an entrepreneur, I can't afford to stop learning. I have a list of podcasts, audiobooks, and more, ready to go while I drive, visit the gym, have lunch, etc. If I have five minutes between meetings, I am going to use that free time to research something online related to my goals or at least think creatively about something I am trying to accomplish and what I could do to draw closer to that goal.

It's about maximizing each day the best I can. It's about creating habits that help me and overcome addictions that distract me. You get better at this over time, but you must start somewhere.

Avoiding Financial Pitfalls

It has taken us awhile, but we are finally here—money talk. Sadly, bringing your unique purpose to life will cost you many things, one of which is money. This is where we sit down and figure out exactly how much money your journey down this path is going to cost you, and what you need to do to prepare for it.

There are two steps involved in this process:

1. A cost analysis.
2. A plan.

Let's jump right in.

1. Cost Analysis

There are costs associated with both your purpose statement and your twelve-week goals. Here is an example list of some costs that I'm talking about:

Education – school, conferences, books, online learning, etc.

Equipment – supplies of any kind that you need to purchase.

Services – You may need to hire an expert in a specific area up front, to help you get off the ground.

Time – If you have a job, you are trading time for money. If you need more time to develop your purpose, but can't afford to give up any of the time you have at work, you need to find a job where you can earn the same, if not more, money with less time. You need to give yourself a raise. (More on this in a minute.)

Using the chart below, begin to research and map out all the projected costs over a three-year period, and then focus on those that are relevant to the next twelve months.

If costs are within your reach, meaning you can already afford all the resources you need, great! Will that be the case in year five or ten as well? If not, adjust the timeline, and look at more of those long-term costs.

Whatever number you come up with, add another 20%. Life always costs more than we think it does, and it's better to be more prepared than surprised.

Projected Costs

Cost Item	Amount

Now look at your first twelve-month costs only and divide that number by the amount of discretionary income you have each month that can help pay for these resources. Discretionary income is the average amount of money you have remaining each month after all necessary items like food, rent, transportation, etc., are paid. You spend discretionary money on luxury items, vacations, entertainment, extra clothing ... things that are not needed but wanted.

Example:

You are twenty-two, going to school part time, and working thirty hours a week. You average about $12 per hour at work and pick up a few small gigs like babysitting each month. So, your net income after taxes is about $1300 per month.

You have taken a look at your bank statements over the last three months, and determined you have about $150 per month in discretionary income, perhaps more if you don't go out to eat as much.

To execute your plan in pursuing your unique purpose, you will need about $10,000, or at least that is what you are estimating, by completing the cost analysis above. So, it looks like this:

$$\frac{\text{Your Net Income} = \$1300 - \text{All Your Bills}}{\$150 \text{ (Discretionary Income)}}$$

Your Twelve-Month Financial Goal of $10,000 ÷ 12 = $833.33 per month needed.

$833.33 - $150 (of Discretionary Income) = $683.33

It looks like you need an additional $683 per month in discretionary income to finance the path you want to go down. What are your options?

2. The Plan

You are going to need to be creative. I am going to throw out some ideas for you to consider, and you will judge which might be doable for you. If they are doable, assign a monthly dollar value to each category. You need to put together a plan that amounts to an extra

$683 a month, using my example above, or whatever that number is for you based on your own estimations.

- **Budget better.** Next to rent, food is the largest expense people have each month. How much money can you save by adjusting either your living situation or eating habits?
$ _____
- **Find another job.** Your low-paying job should be a threat on your SWOT assessment. I know you feel like this is not your best option, but it is. In fact, I have so much to say on this topic that I had to devote a separate section to it, which we will examine more next. For now, let's just imagine you are capable of a 10% raise. Put that number here.
$ _____
- **Pick up a side job.** With an additional five hours per week, could your automobile become a source of revenue as a taxi or delivery person? Could you do side work for a family member or friend? Could you pick up another job somewhere? Could you babysit or walk dogs? If this were the Great Depression, and you had to get creative, what could you do to bring in some extra income?
$ _____
- **Borrow stuff.** Go back and look at your costs. Does everything have to be purchased? Is there anything on this list that you could borrow? Maybe there is, but you don't know who has it. Ask! This is where that networking thing comes into play. Ask—and keep asking. If you were to borrow a few items on your list, what would that save you per month?
$ _____
- **Scholarships/Grants.** Have you looked into all the possible free money that is available? You might be surprised what you qualify for. If education is a line item in your cost analysis, spend time researching scholarships. Ask school counselors. Even localized conferences or workshops might consider scholarshipping you, if you put a good case together for them. It's a wildcard, but what would even a small scholarship save you?
$ _____
- **Strategic partnerships.** In the process of building your team, did you run into anyone that shares your similar passion? Would it be possible to network and find someone who wants to do what you want to do and partner together, so you can share resources? This is one of many reasons why nothing great is ever accomplished alone. What would you save every month by finding a strategic partner?
$ _____

This is not a comprehensive list. Our goal is to pump the well of your creativity. Even if you came up with one idea that could save you some money, you are making progress. If you get stuck here, get others more experienced than yourself involved. Money will prevent you from doing lots of things in this world if you let it.

If you are fighting to bring something you deeply care about to life, you won't let money get in the way. You will not stop until you figure this out, because if you don't, you know you will regret not giving this everything you got.

In our experience, most people know they can make more money somewhere other than where they are now, but they just feel stuck. Even if that is not you, we encourage you to go through this next topic because it will help you better guide those around you that are stuck.

How to Transition from Your Current Job

There are lots of reasons people feel stuck at their job. See if any of these resonate with you right now:

- You don't feel you have the skills to do anything else.
- You don't know what else you even would want to do.
- You feel you should wait it out, because things might change.
- You feel you owe your current employer loyalty.
- You are comfortable where you are and don't want to risk leaving.
- You don't know how to find another job with your skills and experience.

Uncertainty, doubt, fear—we get it. Who hasn't been there? You know what they all have in common?

They are terrible reasons to stay at your job!!

Most people never step into the things they were made for because they are too busy settling for what they already have. You don't want to settle—which is why you are reading this book—but you also don't want to risk leaving only to fail.

That's ultimately the problem: **failure is part of the success equation.** As we have already emphasized, you can't achieve anything meaningful without risking failure. The first thing you have to decide to do when it comes to your current job is take risks. Once you commit to push through your fear, you must learn how to take the right risks.

In search of more funds to finance the development of your unique purpose, here are "Dos & Don'ts" that can help you transition out of your job and find something more beneficial to what you want to achieve.

DO:
- Identify what you need to make per hour and the types of jobs that pay that.
- Narrow your job search to three potential types of jobs that match your financial criteria.
- Create three versions of your résumé that are geared toward each of these jobs.
- Network your butt off, having conversations about your new job search with at least five people per day.
- Set aside time every week to ask employers about jobs even if there is no job posting. Some of the best jobs are landed when you just happen to be in the right place at the right time.

DON'T:
- Send your résumé to any job or manager you have not communicated with.
- Take a commission-only job, unless you have spoken to sales people at that job and are confident that even the worst sales people are making money.
- Quit your job, until you have a starting date confirmed for your next one.
- Network with friends sitting at dead end jobs—aim higher.

The Three Most Important Factors That Will Land a Better Job

1. Networking
This has very little to do with your work experience and much more to do with who you know and what they think you are capable of. All of us know at least one hundred people online through either LinkedIn, Facebook, Instagram, etc. Hit them all up and be honest and creative.

When my wife worked at Under Armour, she told me about an entry-level salesperson at another company that was trying to get the attention of an upper-level director in her office. This guy took a selfie of himself kicked back at his desk, shoes off, and feet propped up with his Under Armour socks showing. With a smile and thumbs up, the image he attached to his email to the director simply said, "I'm a big fan."

The director was so impressed with his creativity, he shared the email with his entire sales staff. This guy may have never closed a sale in his life, but his outside-the-box thinking earned him the right to be heard.

When you network with people you know across different industries, you are reaching into their network of people they know in other sectors. If ten out of these one hundred pass your résumé on to someone they know with their stamp of approval—"Jim would be great at ____. Here is his résumé."—you will move yourself to the top of the stack, winning an opportunity to be heard.

2. A Disciplined Job Search

Networking and looking for available opportunities takes time. The process can drag on for months and months if you do not get disciplined about when and how long you plan to search. If all you have is 10:00 p.m. to midnight, then finding a job BECOMES your second job for these two hours every night of the week.

It's hard. It's often discouraging. You will face rejection. However, this is all part of the character-building process that you will carry with you into living out your purpose. What people don't tell you about getting to do the work they love is that it is just as much work, if not more, than the job you are currently stuck with. To get where you want to go, you will have to build discipline and learn to do things that you hate doing. There are no shortcuts.

3. Great Interview Skills

You need to read about interviewing and, if you know any managers that hire, practice mock interviews with them. So much hinges on your ability to impress others in an interview. There are entire books written on this, so make sharpening your interview skills part of the job search process.

The reality is hundreds of people get hired every day who have almost no skills for the job they just got hired for. They navigated around their experience with strong referrals from their network and impressing managers during their interviews. The people that we coach who have trouble landing better jobs are falling far short in at least one of these two areas 100% of the time.

We believe in you. Be creative in how you present yourself and do your best to enjoy the ride.

Learn by Doing

> "For the things we have to learn before we can do them, we learn by doing them."[1]
> **Aristotle**

As we have illustrated, life is one big science experiment. You create an educated hypothesis about something, and then you conduct the experiment. If it doesn't work, you adjust something and try again.

That is exactly what you are doing through this book.

You don't have to stress about getting it all right—because you won't. You just need to get enough of it right and be willing to learn from what didn't go according to plan. It's about adjustments.

At this point in the journey, you have positioned yourself in a better place than perhaps you have ever been in order to chase after what is most meaningful to you.

Now, it is time to commit to putting ideas into actions.
You have more focus and direction now than most people ever have in their entire life. A thousand people may purchase this very book, but the clear majority won't even make it past Step 2 before quitting.

If you got this far, I know you love learning. Now, you must love doing and taking risks just as much.

If we are, in fact, in a war, take a moment to look at what you have just equipped yourself with:

- A unique map of who you were made to be.
- A map of how the enemy will try to take you out (SWOT).
- A short-term and long-term vision of the future.
- A team around you ready to help you succeed.
- A strategic plan to execute.

And, in this final section:

---

1   "A Quote by Aristotle." Goodreads, 2023. https://www.goodreads.com/quotes/4184-for-the-things-we-have-to-learn-before-we-can

- A knowledge of the most important components that will determine your success.

You have the makings of someone who is ready to take the fight to the enemy. The more you put all you've learned into action, the more battle-tested you become. You will not only be leading yourself well, but leading those around you as they watch.

Everyone has some degree of influence, but yours is about to hit another level. Commit to being an action-oriented person—with a "nothing-to-lose attitude"—and you will look back on a life that was lived to its fullest.

And remember, it's not what you are doing that matters most, but who you are as you go that creates the biggest impact in this life. So, now, let's turn to the final step of this journey and look at the most important areas that will determine your ongoing success.

Notes:

Step 5:
Perfect Your Purpose

Step 5: Perfect Your Purpose

Becoming a Student of Life

How many times in life have you felt like you were your own worst enemy? So often, we put ourselves in situations that set us up for failure.

We keep dating the wrong kinds of people, we settle for jobs where we know we won't be happy, we volunteer for things for which we don't have the talent or passion ... on and on it goes.

Increasing our self-awareness is central to our ongoing success, no matter what we set out to do in life. This kind of insight about how we are wired, however, is not automatic. To consistently put yourself in a place where success is likely, you must commit to being a student of yourself, above anything else.

For the first several years of our organization, I spent most of my time trying to do everything. While doing so, I drifted from one of the core strengths that I brought to our mission in the first place—speaking and teaching. When I took the Myers-Briggs Type Indicator for the first time, I was shocked at how much my personality type (INTJ) described me to a T. I discovered that INTJs are often the jack of all trades, and as such, jump into many things they feel they can improve.

The result? Stretching myself too thin and not operating inside of my core strengths. Developing my ability to delegate and build up the people around me was going to be important if I wanted to be successful.

So, what about you? How can you build habits that demonstrate you are committed to focusing on growing yourself—personally, professionally, and even spiritually?

Consider These Three Habits as Central to Your Future Success:

1. **Establish quarterly learning goals.** I'm sure there are hundreds of things you would like to learn or do better, but which one is most important to your current quarterly goals? Don't overload yourself with learning goals. If you do, you fail to become a

practitioner and are at risk of acquiring knowledge you may never actually use.

Maybe you have determined that you have a great blog you want to get in front of a target audience. Your quarterly learning goals should be to pick a marketing strategy you want to master and dive into acquiring that skill.

2. **Invite steady feedback and evaluation into your life.** Your ability to be humble and invite healthy critique into your life will never become easy.

   We are good at beating ourselves up when we fall short, so it doesn't feel like there is much benefit to inviting others to that party—but there is. Remember the section on putting a solid team of people around you?

   Don't let a twelve-week period go by where you have not invited someone's feedback into the most important areas you are focusing on. It's often painful, sometimes encouraging, but more importantly, it is a necessary part of your commitment to personal growth and doing things with excellence.

3. **When have a you win, figure out what exactly you did right.** When something goes wrong, we are quick to point the finger or launch an investigation into what happened. We want to know where we failed and make sure it doesn't happen again. Ironically, we rarely do this when something goes right. If we don't know what we did well when something good happens, how can we ever repeat it? Thinking a win was attributed to something that had little impact on the outcome could be a costly mistake.

   We could give thousands of examples here, but you don't need them. You just need to remember that people and organizations who win consistently, do so because they are extremely self-aware and take the time to investigate why things work as much as they investigate why they don't. It's a critical healthy habit that all of us are capable of.

At this point, does it feel like there is so much you must get right to be successful? I think about this almost every day. Leading yourself well is an intense balancing act. There are so many things that contribute to success. You must remember that not all things are weighted equally, and you will never be excellent at everything.

One of the main ideas behind Tom Rath's *StrengthsFinder* series is the reality that we will never be excellent at everything, so it makes sense to take what we already do well and invest in doing it even better.

What if, in our earlier example of making marketing a learning goal, you realized that this is something that just does not come naturally to you? In that case, you should begin to develop a plan to have someone else take over in this area. Sure, it may cost you more time and money, but it may also free you to invest in areas that can make you an expert in your field.

Before you move on, ask yourself if you have a genuine plan in place to execute these three key habits of self-awareness and development. Document your plan here.

--- **Notes** ---

Things That Take Most People Out

In coaching people of all ages, we come across several recurring themes that tend to stop someone's progress, if not take them out altogether. This is nothing new. You have been battling them your whole life. Like a big game of Whack-a-Mole, these things pop up and you must see them and respond quickly to win.

In no specific order, here are the most common things that take most people out in the pursuit of purpose.

Losing Streaks

A losing streak is normally a string of negative events we experience over a period of time. Most of us recover from a bad day or two but a losing streak is normally more painful than that.

When most things you invest in are not panning out, doubt flares up and you feel your mind and heart beginning to give up. Negative self-talk becomes louder. The war over your mind, body, and spirit is at a peak.

What can you do when this happens?

My father loved Kenny Rogers and made me listen to one song, "The Gambler," over and over. You have to know when to walk away from the hand you have!

Losing streaks can sometimes be just bad luck. More than likely, they are a sign that something is off in your strategy. You may FEEL like folding; however, the wisest move is to HOLD. Launch an investigation into everything (and I mean EVERYTHING) that has been negative and invite your team into the mix to help troubleshoot with you.

At minimum, you will come up with some areas that may be contributing to your losses and have now put yourself in a position to adjust and try again. If the demon of negative self-talk feels too strong and you just can't find the motivation to keep going, then you need to pause all your efforts and find an exorcist. I am a big believer in counseling. In fact, I think everyone on the planet needs it, so the wisest move you can make might be to seek support from other professionals.

Bottom line, you must be mentally and spiritually strong to tackle developing your unique purpose over the long haul. Expect losing streaks. They are a normal part of the journey. When they happen, evaluate the losses, adjust your strategy, and do whatever it takes to stay mentally and spiritually healthy.

Bloodsuckers

In Jon Gordon's book, *The Energy Bus*, he spends time talking about the impact that negativity has on our ability to get things done. When some of the people closest to us tend to only focus on how we might fail, what we are doing wrong and why things will never get better, they are sucking the passion and drive out of us.

Gordon calls these people "Energy Vampires" and warns that we must not waste time removing them from the bus.

Of course, you can't confuse these bloodsuckers with people who generally do want to see you succeed and yet, are not shy about delivering to you the hard truths. The bloodsuckers you are on the lookout for are the ones that continually suck the wind out of your sails. You need to identify the patterns and be quick to separate yourself from their involvement.

Easier said than done, right? What if it's a spouse, boss, or best friend?

You need to work up the courage to have an honest heart-to-heart with them. Tell them how you feel and how their words or actions are impacting you. If you have tried to communicate these kinds of things in the past, do it again. And again. And again. Each time you do, you show resolve to not fall victim to opinions that are derailing you, no matter how important those voices are to you.

If you build a habit of remaining silent in these situations, you are just hurting yourself. You bottle up resentment until one day you either quit or erupt. Instead, be quick to address the negativity as it arises and let people around you know that you are a person that refuses to be taken out by the opinion of others.

No, this is not easy and that's exactly why it takes so many people out. Now you are aware it's a real threat, so put a strategy in place as to how you will handle bloodsuckers when they show up. If it doesn't work, try something else. Keep adjusting and talk to others who have overcome this adversity in their journey. Eventually you will land on a system that works for you. And read Gordon's book; it's a good one.

Marathons

The very thought of running a marathon seems miserable. Yeah, it would be cool to say I did it but it just seems like unnecessary self-torture to me. If you are a long-distance runner, I'm sure you understand the amount of focus and training it takes to complete. The rest of us don't even consider the thought of it because we are so far out of shape in this area.

When a person decides they want to pursue their unique design, something that is of great passion and worth to them, they generally start out at a pace they cannot maintain over the long haul. Most people never make it out of the discovery phase.

When you said "yes" to embracing who you are uniquely made you to be, you signed up for a race not marked by distance, but by time. Were you intending on just dabbling in your passion or were you setting out to make a meaningful impact on the lives of others? You are either committing to developing your unique purpose for the rest of your life or you are fine just settling for average.

As a Christian, I believe in the idea of sanctification. It's just a fancy church word that means I am in the process of modeling my life after Jesus. It's a process that I will never fully achieve until I get to heaven, but that doesn't stop me from making progress. When other Christians let me down, I remember that they too are in the process of sanctification and are no better or worse off than me. Progress is slow, painful, and includes setbacks, but it's still progress if I can stay focused on the long-term goal.

Long-distance runners, Christians, and so many other types of people on this earth must adapt to being clearly focused on their long-term goals to endure the difficulties they will encounter in reaching their destination. The way you do this is by establishing healthy rhythms in your life that can sustain you.

You are going to have bursts of energy or passion along the way. Other legs of this race will seem dry and mundane. Healthy rhythms can help you build stamina, so let's look at a few ways to do that:

- Establish a weekly rhythm of nutrition and exercise. Your body is a one of one; you don't own a spare.
- Build in frequent short breaks in the week and longer ones every few months. Like a swimmer, you must come up for air to keep going.
- Begin and end your day with thanksgiving. I mentioned this as part of my core strategy before. It will help you stay focused on the positive.
- Choose an object that will help you keep the end in mind. For me, it's a simple print out of my legacy vision. I look at it before I plan my week and have done so for years.
- Set aside time to think on a weekly basis. There are different types of thinking—creative, strategic, meditation, etc. Hit the pause button and zoom out. It's a great habit to get into that allows you to reset your mind and focus on what matters most.

Okay, we are not going to list every healthy habit imaginable. You know yourself. What habits are important for you to build to not be taken out by Losing Streaks, Bloodsuckers, and Marathons? Throw your thoughts down here.

My Key Healthy Habits

Embracing Failure and Adversity

It feels like we have already talked about this a ton, doesn't it? Well, there is something I have been wanting to say but have been waiting until close to the end before doing so. I wanted to save the most encouraging and inspiring stuff for this very moment, so here it goes....

You are a pro at embracing failure AND resilience.

Let's look at some areas where you have fallen short in life, up to this point:

- You have lied to people.
- You have talked trash about people behind their back.
- You have taken things that do not belong to you.
- You have been insensitive at times.
- You have used words to tear people down rather than build them up.
- You have implemented ideas that didn't work out.
- You have made a judgment about someone and been wrong.
- You have quit on things too soon.
- You have let people around you down.

And this is just the warm-up.

You can keep going for another few pages if you feel inspired to. You have screwed up a ton.

And yet, you are still here. Alive. Seeking to make the most out of this life you have been given. Despite your epic failures, you still have hope.

And hope keeps us moving forward even when the reality of potential failure looms. We call this resilience, and it is the character trait that will lead you toward breakthrough.

While failure in some form is imminent yet again in our lives, we can remain confident and optimistic because we also have a track record of bouncing back no matter what life throws at us. Humility cannot exist without failure and humility is the secret ingredient to navigating through this rollercoaster of life.

Failure fuels the resolve of the humble and resilient in the following ways:

- It protects us from arrogance.
- It tests our faith.
- It brings to light areas you are weak in.
- It builds our character.
- It exposes our fear.
- It inspires honest evaluation.
- It teaches us patience.
- It strengthens our strategy.

Failure is life's most proficient teacher. Its lessons are painful, but the absence of its education would be far more damaging.

Failure is the best friend you always wanted but never had. It is here to ultimately remind you once again that success in this life is not about what you are doing, but who you are being.

This world is longing for courageous men and women who are not afraid to fail. Failure is an event, not a medical condition. There are several epic failures still scheduled for your life and no matter how conservatively you live, you won't be able to avoid them.

Your best course of action is to let failure do what it was designed to do—toughen you up for the war you find yourself in. There is no room for victim mentalities on this train. Bad stuff happens to good people all the time; you are not immune to it. You will either make the most out of what you must work with or spend the rest of your life being sad and angry about what could have been.

Embrace adversity by choosing to be thankful for the things it's intending to produce in you. If you forget what those are, read through the list above again. Now add to the list by taking time to list out the positive things that your past failures have drawn out of you.

Failure Is My Friend

Past Failure	Redeeming Value

How to Stay Focused and Motivated

Your ability to stay focused and motivated on this journey is the fire you want to kindle. We want to highlight some ideas that we think will help; however, this is something you must continue to experiment with over time. Reflect on times in your life when you have been most motivated and make a note of why you think that was the case.

What Motivates Me	
I was motivated when...	Because...

Study Your Motivational Patterns

The list of motivators that exists in life is extensive. The book *What Motivates Me*, by Adrian Gostick and Chester Elton, is one of many great resources you can find on this topic. Understanding your motivational patterns should be part of your learning goals at some point. Review some of the motivators you identified with in Step 2.

If you are motivated by impacting others, for example, you should measure your progress not by money or recognition, but by the stories you encounter of people you have helped. Everyone is motivated by something. When you pinpoint yours, make sure you think through how to create some goals around these motivators. Here are three tips for keeping yourself focused and motivated:

1. Create an Inspiration Room

An inspiration room is an area in your home or office that inspires you to stay focused on your goals. Not everyone can afford to designate an entire room to something like this but at least a desk area or wall is better than nothing.

In my inspiration room, I have movie posters that symbolize the level of risk and sacrifice it takes to bring something you are truly passionate about to life. I also have memorabilia in the form of pictures and letters from lives impacted. I encountered a homeless man in California selling his homeless signs to pedestrians walking by. I was so impressed with his creativity that I bought his cardboard sign for $20 and placed it above my desk to remind me of the power of innovation.

When you design your inspiration space, it should remind you of the big picture in life. It should highlight victories, cultivate hope, and draw out the creative within you. Try it. Send us a picture when you're done too. We would love to be inspired alongside you.

2. Journal

I'm kind of bad at this but I can tell you that pulling out my journal and reading the few entries that do exist is motivating to me. On a personal note, my journal has helped me see the evidence of God's existence. I have recorded dreams that have become reality and words that were spoken over me by strangers who didn't know me but were dead accurate. I even documented some of my deepest prayers and have seen many answered.

Documenting the journey will help you remember that the sacrifice is worth it. You can push through your current affliction because you have before. Circumstances always change over time and a journal can be the perfect testament to that.

You don't have to journal every day. Start by doing it once a month for a year. If it helps, awesome. If not, at least you will have some amazing insight waiting to be discovered by future generations when you check out.

3. Calculate Regret

I have a go-to question I ask myself every time motivation is running low. If I stop doing what I'm doing right now, will I regret not persevering through later in life?

If my answer is yes, I let the fear of regret motivate me forward.

We can't go back, only forward, so we all must make choices today about how we want to live. As I said earlier in this project, we will all acquire some level of regret. My goal is to not accumulate any more of it than necessary.

I'm sure you are about tapped out on thinking about strategy, evaluating every area of your life, and just thinking in general. It's exhausting.

I have one last thought I want to leave you with before you are ready to fly on your own, so let's finish strong together and take this next topic to heart.

Enjoying the Ride

We have more than likely not met in person, but I do mean this with deep sincerity: I am so proud of you. You don't realize how few people make it this far, but it's true. You are among a minority of people with the ambition needed to be someone special. At this point, you don't even have to achieve a single goal you set, and you will still impact people around you because you have the courage to travel down a path that they only dream about.

You are taking risks and you will fail your way forward. Most everyone around you will exert their energy trying to avoid failure, only to find that in their conservative approach, they still fail.

Your level of confidence and doubt may seesaw, but your daily choice to keep learning and moving will be the foundation of your success.

If you want to perfect your purpose, there is one thing left to do—enjoy the ride. Joy is something we can choose to experience when we give thanks for this life. The wealthiest, most famous individuals to walk this earth have never been able to find lasting contentment in fame or fortune. That is never going to change.

If what you are setting out to do is primarily self-serving, you are in for major disappointment. However, if you desire to take the things you have been blessed with and offer them back to others for the good of those around you, you cannot fail.

In the words of one of the richest, wisest kings ever known:

> "I perceived that there is nothing better for them than to be joyful and to do good as long as they live; also that everyone

> should eat and drink and take pleasure in all his toil—
> this is God's gift to man."
> **Solomon, Ecclesiastes 3:12-13 ESV**

Since we lack the ability to control all our circumstances, it makes sense to develop the things we can control and learn to enjoy the ride along the way with everything else. I must make the decision every morning to enjoy the unpredictability of life. It would be futile to fight against it. So, like you, I will move on from the writing of this book and begin to execute my plan. Not everything will work out as I hope and that's okay. One thing I know for sure, I will never regret trying.

And neither will you.

Notes:

SAVE TIME. ACHIEVE CLARITY. MAXIMIZE YOUR IMPACT.

Private workshops that help you gain clarity, make a transition, or find purpose.

Our Purpose Project Workshop will fast-track your personal and professional success by...

IDENTIFYING YOUR UNTAPPED POTENTIAL

ESTABLISHING YOUR KEY SUCCESS FACTORS

CLARIFYING & SIMPLIFYING YOUR STRATEGIC PATH

BRINGING FOCUS TO YOUR COMPETITIVE ADVANTAGE

Joe Elliott is the founder and executive director of The Catalyst Collective, a non-profit based in Austin, Texas, whose mission is to help the next generation find clarity and confidence around their unique design and purpose. His organization reaches thousands of students and adults across the US with its innovative approach to decoding individual design and guiding people forward. Joe and his network of certified Purpose Project Guides are available to assist you beyond just the blueprint provided in this book. You can learn more at www.purposepro.org.

www.ingramcontent.com/pod-product-compliance
Lightning Source LLC
Chambersburg PA
CBHW050512240426
43673CB00004B/197